AF815505

Published by Offord & Associates Real Estate LLC
Email: info@kimberlyofford.com
www.kimberlyofford.com

RECIPE FOR
REFERRALS

A COMPLETE PLANNER FOR GENERATING REFERRALS

THE ADVANCED COMPANION TO
"WORK FOR THE REFERRALS, NOT THE COMMISSION"

Offord & Associates Real Estate LLC
www.kimberlyofford.com

Recipe for Referrals

Thanks for using this resource to write your own recipe for referrals!

My name is Kimberly Offord and I am so excited to share the companion workbook for, "Work for the Referral, Not the Commission." In the first workbook, my goal was to supplement and eventually replace your current marketing with a solid referral based business. I hope that you were able to move closer to that goal.

Now, the advanced planning guide, "Recipe for Referrals" is here to grow your referral business even more. This guide will provide you with more weekly and quarterly planners to try. In addition to the samples provided in this workbook, try other combinations to get the right number of referrals flowing into your business.

By making this planner a part of your daily routine, you will become an expert at referrals in no time. Be sure to share this resource with other real estate agents in your brokerage. I want each of you to be successful with a business that keeps giving.

Remember, "work for the referral and not the commission!"

Kimberly Offord

Kimberly Offord
IL Licensed REALTOR®
Real Estate Coach, Author

RECIPE FOR REFERRALS

INCLUDED IN THIS WORKBOOK

- Annual Goal Worksheet (Setting Goals)
- The Essential Ingredients for Referrals
- The Core Plan Explained
- Quarterly Plan (Recipe) Explained
- Quarterly Budget Worksheet
- 8 Sample Quarterly Plans (Recipes)
- Quarterly Opportunity Identifier
- Quarterly Plan Worksheet
- 52 Weekly Planners

Setting Goals

Now that referrals will become a significant contributor to your overall marketing goals, set quantitive goals. Think of how your referral business can supplement and eventually replace your traditional lead generation system.

Business Planning

1. What are your overall financial goals for this year? Dream Big!

2. What is the average price of properties in your market?

3. What is your average commission percentage earned per sale?

4. Multiply line 3 by line 2. Then factor in fees and commission splits. This is your average earnings per sale.

5. Divide Line 1 by line 4. This is the number of closing you will need to reach your financial goals for this year.

Referral Projected Goals

6. Total number of contacts you have in your database/CRM system.

7. Multiply the number of contacts by 10%. This is the goal number of contacts that will send you referral business.

8. What percentage of your leads close? Multiply line 7 by the appropriate percentage. This is the number of referral deals you could close this year.

9. Multiply line 8 by line 4. This is your income earned from referral business alone.

The Essential Ingredients for Referrals

Database

The heart of your referral campaign is your database. Build a solid list of people who know, like and trust you. This is your sphere of influence. Your sphere could include, family, friends, past and current clients and/or service partners. Remember: Quality over Quantity. It is better to have a list of 100 people who will refer you versus a list of 1,000 people who will not. Use a CRM system to house your database.

Direct Mail

Direct mail will be the backbone of your direct mail campaign. Personalized mailers should be sent periodically throughout the year to generate referral business. Some examples include:

- Postcards, Promotional Letters
- Handwritten Notes, Holiday Cards

Personal Touch

Think of unique personalized ways to stay front of mind. For example:

- Invitations to coffee or lunch
- Care packages
- Customer appreciation events
- Phone Calls

The Essential Ingredients for Referrals

Social Media

Social media is one of the easiest and FREE ways to stay top of mind within your sphere of influence. Here are a few tips:

- Follow your contacts on social media, celebrate their anniversaries, wish them happy birthday, interact on posts.
- Post often about real estate, your niche market and personal interests. Post live and recorded video.
- Establish a business page on your preferred social media.
- Understand which social media platforms are best for you.
- Understand which social media platforms are used by your sphere.
- Be consistent, use hashtags and always ASK for referrals.
- Schedule social media posts in advance with syndication aps.
- Join social media groups to network with real estate agents in other markets. They are a great source for referral income.

Email & Text Messaging

With the ability to send text messages and other innovative forms of communication, email marketing doesn't have the same reach as it once did. However, it should not be ignored. Use email to support other efforts.

- Drip Campaigns (Email & Text)
- Email Newsletters
- Market Reports and Property Searches

The Essential Ingredients for Referrals

Community Involvement

Get involved in causes that matter to you. Give the same support you are seeking to local businesses and nonprofits. Become the involved neighborhood expert of your chosen community. Refer other service providers to your friends and loved ones. Get involved in the real estate community! Network with Realtors in other cities and niche' markets. Remember, **referrals are a gift that keeps giving.**

NOTES

The Core Plan

At a minimum, target 75-100 people in your sphere (friends, family, past clients, service partners). This will be the CORE group. Follow the touch plan for 12 months.

Touch Goal ⟶ 16 Touches A Quarter (3 Months)

Social Media
Daily Activity

Post to social media **at least** 3x's a week (Everyday life, information, celebrations, sales, inspiration, post interactions, live/recorded video, stories etc)

Direct Mail
At Least 1 Mailing A Quarter

Schedule **at least** 1 mass mailing to your core sphere group during the quarter (Post Card, Handwritten Note or Holiday Card)

Personal Touch
Weekly Activity

Call at least 5-10 people in Sphere of Influence weekly. Invite to lunch or coffee, send dinner gift card, ask for referrals

Email/Text
Monthly Activity

Set up a drip campaign within your CRM system. Be careful not to spam anyone with unwanted email. Provide valuable information.

Community Involvement
Monthly Activity

To get referrals, you must give referrals. Highlight or refer at least 4 businesses or service partners every month.

Remember the goal is to build a referral based business while also building your database with people who KNOW, LIKE and TRUST you.

Quarterly Goals

GOAL 1: Implement the CORE Activities

Core Activities = Consistent Activities

- Post on Social Media 3xs a week.
- Call 2-5 Contacts in Sphere of Influence a week.
- Refer business to at least 12 other service partners or local businesses during the quarter (3 months).
- Send one direct mail piece to Sphere of Influence a quarter.
- Make contact with another Real Estate agent in a different market once a quarter.

On the following sample quarter recipes, Core activities will be identified with the letter **C**.

GOAL 2: Your Pick (Activities of Your Choice)

- Pick 4 other touch points to implement any time during the quarter.

Decide on four additional ways you will touch your audience during the quarter to encourage referrals and stay front of mind. These activities can be performed daily, weekly or monthly. **At the very least each four should be performed monthly.**

On the following sample quarter recipes, "your pick" activities will be identified with the letter **P**.

NOW, lets get started formulating our quarterly plans (recipes).

ANNUAL BUDGET

Most of the suggested activities to get referrals are free, however there will be some that require a financial investment.

***Remember, this budget only addresses referral based business building. Total marketing budget should be calculated with your annual business plan.**

DIRECT MAIL
Postcards, Letters, Greeting Cards etc) $________

POSTAGE $________

SPHERE APPRECIATION
(Coffee, Lunch, Dinner, Care Packages etc) $________

HOLIDAYS & CELEBRATIONS
(Birthdays, Anniversaries, Weddings, Cards, Gifts, etc) $________

PRINT MATERIAL
(Flyers, Business Cards etc) $________

CMS/CRM
(Contact Management System also factored into main marketing budget) $________

SPECIAL EVENTS $________

MISCELLANEOUS $________

TOTAL BUDGET $________

8

REFERRAL RECIPES

Sample Plans

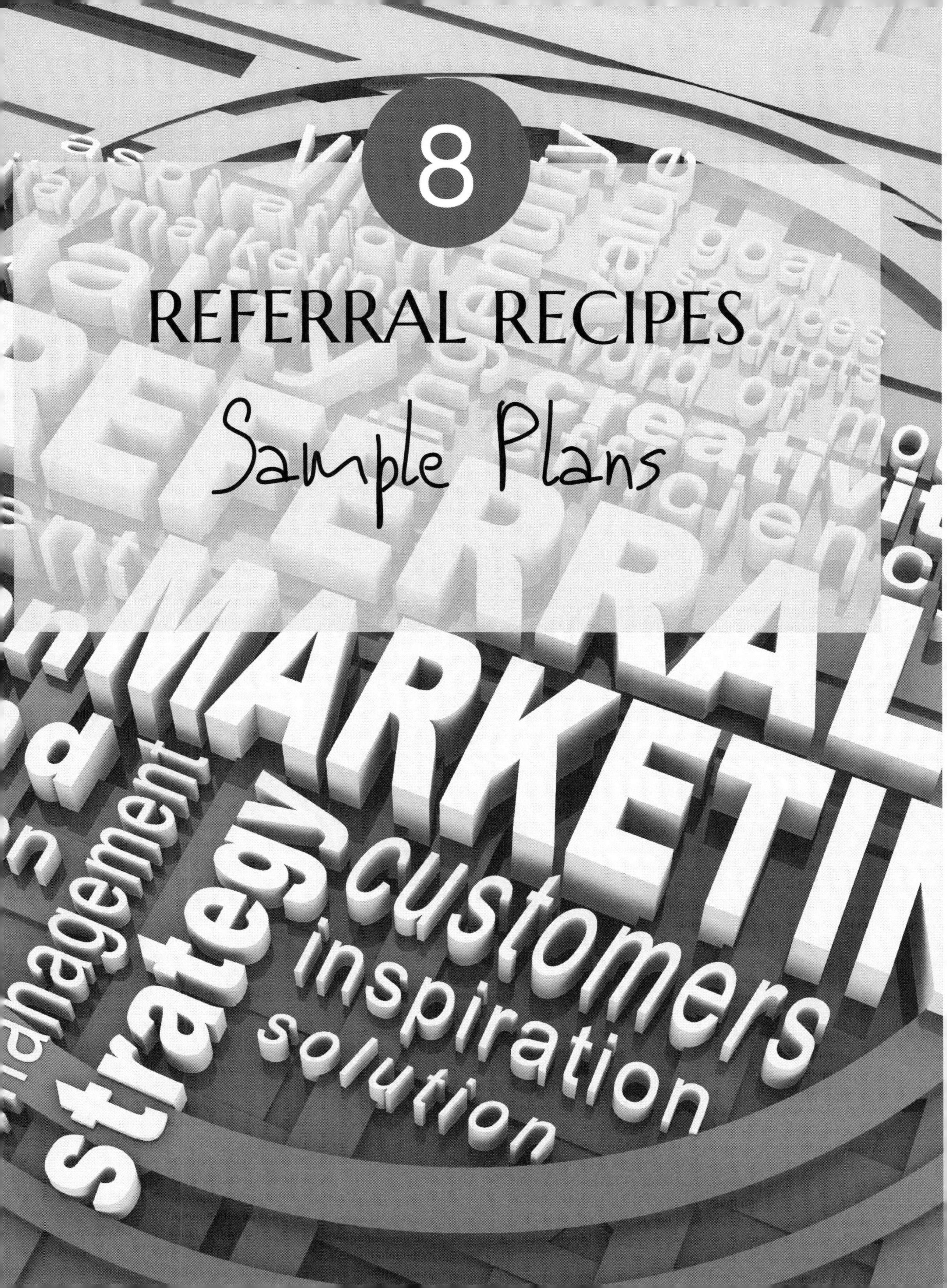

SAMPLE RECIPE 1:
Quarterly Activities

Remember: C = Core & P = Your Pick

Touch Goal ⟶ At Least 16 Touches A Quarter

Social Media	Direct Mail	Personal Touch
C - Post to Facebook 3xs a week. C - Respond to post comments daily P - Post pictures to Instagram weekly (personal & professional) P - Join and post to a real estate related community 3xs a week	C - Send a promo postcard to Sphere of Influence with a call to action & ask for referrals 1x a month. P - Send celebratory cards - birthday, anniversaries etc.	C - Call 5 - 10 people in your sphere a week and ask for referrals.
Email & Text	**Database**	**Community Involvement**
P - Set up a drip campaign for your sphere of influence to receive 1 email a month (various topics) - ask for referrals	C - Ask previous clients if they know anyone in need of your services - Add to database. C - Add contacts from open houses, seminars etc. to database	C - Refer 1 business or service partner a week C - Make contact and personal introduction to a Real estate agent in another market. (1 or more per qtr.)

SAMPLE RECIPE 2:
Quarterly Activities

Remember: C = Core & P = Your Pick

Touch Goal ⟶ At Least 16 Touches A Quarter

Social Media	Direct Mail	Personal Touch
C - Post to Social Media 3xs a week. (personal & real estate related) C - Respond to post comments daily P - Go Live on a Social Media Platform at least 1x a week	C - Send a market report mailing to Sphere of Influence with a call to action & ask for referrals 1x a month.	C - Call 5 - 10 people in your sphere a week and ask for referrals. P - Call and Invite at least 5 people in your sphere to coffee during the quarter.
Email & Text	**Database**	**Community Involvement**
P - Send a monthly email newsletter to your mailing list	C - Ask previous clients if they know anyone in need of your services - Add to database. C - Add contacts from open houses, seminars etc. to database P - Add an email sign up link to your social profiles.	C - Refer 1 business or service partner a week C - Make contact and personal introduction to a Real estate agent in another market. (1 or more per qtr.) P - Volunteer to organize a neighborhood clean-up in your community.

SAMPLE RECIPE 3:
Quarterly Activities

Remember: C = Core & P = Your Pick

Touch Goal ⟶ At Least 16 Touches A Quarter

Social Media	Direct Mail	Personal Touch
C - Post to Social Media 3xs a week. (personal & real estate related) C - Respond to post comments daily P - Go live on Social Media - Interview a Lender, Attorney and Home Inspector (1 a month)	C - Send a monthly food recipe card to Sphere of Influence with a call to action & ask for referrals 1x a month.	C - Call 5 - 10 people in your sphere a week and ask for referrals. P - Drop off flowers, seeds and/or a plant to past clients for spring planting. - Include a business card and ask for referrals.
Email & Text	**Database**	**Community Involvement**
P - Set up home owners to get monthly email market reports.	C - Ask previous clients if they know anyone in need of your services - Add to database. C - Add contacts from open houses, seminars etc. to database P - Create a landing page to capture email leads	C - Refer 1 business or service partner a week C - Make contact and personal introduction to a Real estate agent in another market. (1 or more per qtr.) P - Host a free Investment seminar

SAMPLE RECIPE 4:
Quarterly Activities

Remember: C = Core & P = Your Pick

Touch Goal ⟶ At Least 16 Touches A Quarter

Social Media	Direct Mail	Personal Touch
C - Post to Social Media 3xs a week. (personal & real estate related) C - Respond to post comments daily P - Go live at a listing- give a virtual tour	C - Send a handwritten note to your contact list asking for referrals	C - Call 5 - 10 people in your sphere a week and ask for referrals. P - Host a client appreciation event
Email & Text	**Database**	**Community Involvement**
P - Send a text message announcing a new listing P - Send a video message email to your clients that provide helpful information	C - Ask previous clients if they know anyone in need of your services. - Add to database. C - Add contacts from open houses, seminars etc. to database P - Ask contacts for service providers like plumbers, electricians, lawn maintenance providers etc that you can add to your database.	C - Refer 1 business or service partner a week C - Make contact and personal introduction to a Real estate agent in another market. (1 or more per qtr.) P - Volunteer to work on a committee with your local association

SAMPLE RECIPE 5:
Quarterly Activities

Remember: C = Core & P = Your Pick

Touch Goal ⟶ At Least 16 Touches A Quarter

Social Media	Direct Mail	Personal Touch
C - Post to Social Media 3xs a week. (personal & real estate related) C - Respond to post comments daily P - Do a Social Media video or story featuring a neighborhood attraction (1x each month)	C - Send a handwritten holiday cards to your contact list asking for referrals	C - Call 5 - 10 people in your sphere a week and ask for referrals. P - Hand deliver holiday gift to selct number in Sphere of Influence
Email & Text	**Database**	**Community Involvement**
P - Send an email featuring all of your Brokerage listings only (1x each month).	C - Ask previous clients if they know anyone in need of your services - Add to database. C - Add contacts from open houses, seminars etc. to database	C - Refer 1 business or service partner a week C - Make contact and personal introduction to a Real estate agent in another market. (1 or more per qtr.) P - Purchase gift certificates for local businesses and gift to clients

SAMPLE RECIPE 6:
Quarterly Activities

Remember: C = Core & P = Your Pick

Touch Goal ⟶ At Least 16 Touches A Quarter

Social Media	Direct Mail	Personal Touch
C - Post to Social Media 3xs a week. (personal & real estate related) C - Respond to post comments daily P - Plan a series of posts featuring home maintenance tips	C - Send a postcard mailing to sphere of influence/ contacts offering a free CMA	C - Call 5 - 10 people in your sphere a week and ask for referrals. P - Make contact with a Realtor in another market where you can provide and receive referrals business
Email & Text	**Database**	**Community Involvement**
P - Change your email signature to include, "I love Referrals" with a contact number.	C - Ask previous clients if they know anyone in need your services. - Add to database. C - Add contacts from open houses, seminars etc. to database	C - Refer 1 business or service partner week C - Make contact and personal introduction to a Real estate agent in another market. (1 or more per qtr.) P - Collect and distribute care packages for the less fortunate- invite sphere of influence to volunteer or assist with collection efforts.

SAMPLE RECIPE 7:
Quarterly Activities

Remember: C = Core & P = Your Pick

Touch Goal ⟶ At Least 16 Touches A Quarter

Social Media	Direct Mail	Personal Touch
C - Post to Social Media 3xs a week. (personal & real estate related) C - Respond to post comments daily P - Create Social Media stories around a day in teh life of Real Estate	C - Send a newsletter or postcard to your contact list featuring a "Restaurant of the Month"	C - Call 5 - 10 people in your sphere a week and ask for referrals. P - Send Lunch or Dinner to a person in your sphere of influence. (1x a month)
Email & Text	**Database**	**Community Involvement**
P - Send an email to contacts providing information on real estate investment opportunities	C - Ask previous clients if they know anyone in need your services. - Add to database. C - Add contacts from open houses, seminars etc. to database	C - Refer 1 business or service partner week C - Make contact and personal introduction to a Real estate agent in another market. (1 or more per qtr.) P - Join the local Chamber of Commerce

SAMPLE RECIPE 8:
Quarterly Activities

Remember: C = Core & P = Your Pick

Touch Goal ⟶ At Least 16 Touches A Quarter

Social Media	Direct Mail	Personal Touch
C - Post to Social Media 3xs a week. (personal & real estate related) C - Respond to post comments daily P - Post pictures of SOLD properties to Instagram and any other social media accounts	C - Send a "Year in Review" letter to sphere recapping the year in real estate.	C - Call 5 - 10 people in your sphere a week and ask for referrals. P - Give all past and current clients promotional gift with your name (ie pens, cutting boards, glasses etc)
Email & Text	**Database**	**Community Involvement**
P - Send an email to contact list with a featured client of the month. (1x a month)	C - Ask previous clients if they know anyone in need your services - Add to database. C - Add contacts from open houses, seminars etc. to database	C - Refer 1 business or service partner week C - Make contact and personal introduction to a Real estate agent in another market. (1 or more per qtr.) P - Host a community home tour

Quarter 1 Planning

QUARTER 1 OPPORTUNITIES

Plan Opportunities to Touch Your Sphere of Influence in Advance

CELEBRATIONS
(Birthdays, Anniversaries, Weddings etc.)

HOLIDAYS
(Cards, Gifts, Care Packages etc)

SOCIAL MEDIA MARKETING
(Closings, New Listings, Open Houses)

PLANNED TOPICS FOR BLOG POSTS, NEWSLETTERS, EMAILS

MISCELLANEOUS TASKS

RECIPE: Quarter Activities

Remember: C = Core & P = Your Pick

Touch Goal ⟶ At Least 16 Touches A Quarter

Social Media	Direct Mail	Personal Touch
Email & Text	**Database**	**Community Involvement**

WEEKLY PLANNER

Week 1

Date________

MONDAY

TUESDAY

WEDNESDAY

THURSDAY

FRIDAY

SATURDAY

SUNDAY

TO DO

- [ ] Post on Social Media at least 3xs
- [ ] Complete Touch Point Activity
- [ ] Add Contacts to Database
- [ ] Ask for Referrals
- [ ] Review Goals
- [ ] Refer Another Business
- [ ] Plan For Next Week

SPHERE OF INFLUENCE CALLS

1.
2.
3.
4.
5.

NOTES

WEEKLY PLANNER

Week 2

Date________

MONDAY

TUESDAY

WEDNESDAY

THURSDAY

FRIDAY

SATURDAY

SUNDAY

TO DO

- [ ] Post on Social Media at least 3xs
- [ ] Complete Touch Point Activity
- [ ] Add Contacts to Database
- [ ] Ask for Referrals
- [ ] Review Goals
- [ ] Refer Another Business
- [ ] Plan For Next Week

SPHERE OF INFLUENCE CALLS

1.
2.
3.
4.
5.

NOTES

WEEKLY PLANNER

Week 3

Date________

MONDAY

TUESDAY

WEDNESDAY

THURSDAY

FRIDAY

SATURDAY

SUNDAY

TO DO

- [ ] Post on Social Media at least 3xs
- [ ] Complete Touch Point Activity
- [ ] Add Contacts to Database
- [ ] Ask for Referrals
- [ ] Review Goals
- [ ] Refer Another Business
- [ ] Plan For Next Week

SPHERE OF INFLUENCE CALLS

1.
2.
3.
4.
5.

NOTES

WEEKLY PLANNER

Week 4

Date________

MONDAY

TUESDAY

WEDNESDAY

THURSDAY

FRIDAY

SATURDAY

SUNDAY

TO DO

- [ ] Post on Social Media at least 3xs
- [ ] Complete Touch Point Activity
- [ ] Add Contacts to Database
- [ ] Ask for Referrals
- [ ] Review Goals
- [ ] Refer Another Business
- [ ] Plan For Next Week

SPHERE OF INFLUENCE CALLS

1.
2.
3.
4.
5.

NOTES

WEEKLY PLANNER

Week 5

Date________

MONDAY

TUESDAY

WEDNESDAY

THURSDAY

FRIDAY

SATURDAY

SUNDAY

TO DO

- [ ] Post on Social Media at least 3xs
- [ ] Complete Touch Point Activity
- [ ] Add Contacts to Database
- [ ] Ask for Referrals
- [ ] Review Goals
- [ ] Refer Another Business
- [ ] Plan For Next Week

SPHERE OF INFLUENCE CALLS

1.
2.
3.
4.
5.

NOTES

WEEKLY PLANNER

Week 6 Date________

MONDAY

TUESDAY

WEDNESDAY

THURSDAY

FRIDAY

SATURDAY

SUNDAY

TO DO

- [ ] Post on Social Media at least 3xs
- [ ] Complete Touch Point Activity
- [ ] Add Contacts to Database
- [ ] Ask for Referrals
- [ ] Review Goals
- [ ] Refer Another Business
- [ ] Plan For Next Week

SPHERE OF INFLUENCE CALLS

1.
2.
3.
4.
5.

NOTES

WEEKLY PLANNER

Week 7

Date________

MONDAY

TUESDAY

WEDNESDAY

THURSDAY

FRIDAY

SATURDAY

SUNDAY

TO DO

- [ ] Post on Social Media at least 3xs
- [ ] Complete Touch Point Activity
- [ ] Add Contacts to Database
- [ ] Ask for Referrals
- [ ] Review Goals
- [ ] Refer Another Business
- [ ] Plan For Next Week

SPHERE OF INFLUENCE CALLS

1.
2.
3.
4.
5.

NOTES

WEEKLY PLANNER

Week 8

Date________

MONDAY

TUESDAY

WEDNESDAY

THURSDAY

FRIDAY

SATURDAY

SUNDAY

TO DO

- [ ] Post on Social Media at least 3xs
- [ ] Complete Touch Point Activity
- [ ] Add Contacts to Database
- [ ] Ask for Referrals
- [ ] Review Goals
- [ ] Refer Another Business
- [ ] Plan For Next Week

SPHERE OF INFLUENCE CALLS

1.
2.
3.
4.
5.

NOTES

WEEKLY PLANNER

Week 9

Date________

MONDAY

TUESDAY

WEDNESDAY

THURSDAY

FRIDAY

SATURDAY

SUNDAY

TO DO

- [ ] Post on Social Media at least 3xs
- [ ] Complete Touch Point Activity
- [ ] Add Contacts to Database
- [ ] Ask for Referrals
- [ ] Review Goals
- [ ] Refer Another Business
- [ ] Plan For Next Week

SPHERE OF INFLUENCE CALLS

1.
2.
3.
4.
5.

NOTES

WEEKLY PLANNER

Week 10

Date________

MONDAY

TUESDAY

WEDNESDAY

THURSDAY

FRIDAY

SATURDAY

SUNDAY

TO DO

- [ ] Post on Social Media at least 3xs
- [ ] Complete Touch Point Activity
- [ ] Add Contacts to Database
- [ ] Ask for Referrals
- [ ] Review Goals
- [ ] Refer Another Business
- [ ] Plan For Next Week

SPHERE OF INFLUENCE CALLS

1.
2.
3.
4.
5.

NOTES

WEEKLY PLANNER

Week 11

Date________

MONDAY

TUESDAY

WEDNESDAY

THURSDAY

FRIDAY

SATURDAY

SUNDAY

TO DO

- [ ] Post on Social Media at least 3xs
- [ ] Complete Touch Point Activity
- [ ] Add Contacts to Database
- [ ] Ask for Referrals
- [ ] Review Goals
- [ ] Refer Another Business
- [ ] Plan For Next Week

SPHERE OF INFLUENCE CALLS

1.
2.
3.
4.
5.

NOTES

WEEKLY PLANNER

Week 12

Date________

MONDAY

TUESDAY

WEDNESDAY

THURSDAY

FRIDAY

SATURDAY

SUNDAY

TO DO

- [ ] Post on Social Media at least 3xs
- [ ] Complete Touch Point Activity
- [ ] Add Contacts to Database
- [ ] Ask for Referrals
- [ ] Review Goals
- [ ] Refer Another Business
- [ ] Plan For Next Week

SPHERE OF INFLUENCE CALLS

1.
2.
3.
4.
5.

NOTES

WEEKLY PLANNER

Week 13

Date________

MONDAY

TUESDAY

WEDNESDAY

THURSDAY

FRIDAY

SATURDAY

SUNDAY

TO DO

- [ ] Post on Social Media at least 3xs
- [ ] Complete Touch Point Activity
- [ ] Add Contacts to Database
- [ ] Ask for Referrals
- [ ] Review Goals
- [ ] Refer Another Business
- [ ] Plan For Next Week

SPHERE OF INFLUENCE CALLS

1.
2.
3.
4.
5.

NOTES

Quarter 1 Recap

What worked well?

Which activity did you feel most comfortable performing? Why?

Which activity was the least comfortable? Why?

Was it difficult or easy asking for referrals? Why?

How many referral leads did you receive over the past quarter?

Did you meet any new service partners you can refer to your sphere?

Did your database grow?

What adjustments need to be made for the next quarter?

Quarter 2
Planner

QUARTER 2 OPPORTUNITIES

Plan Opportunities to Touch Your Sphere of Influence in Advance

CELEBRATIONS
(Birthdays, Anniversaries, Weddings etc.)

HOLIDAYS
(Cards, Gifts, Care Packages etc)

SOCIAL MEDIA MARKETING
(Closings, New Listings, Open Houses)

PLANNED TOPICS FOR BLOG POSTS, NEWSLETTERS, EMAILS

MISCELLANEOUS TASKS

RECIPE: Quarter Activities

Remember: C = Core & P = Your Pick

Touch Goal ⟶ At Least 16 Touches A Quarter

Social Media	Direct Mail	Personal Touch
Email & Text	**Database**	**Community Involvement**

WEEKLY PLANNER

Week 14

Date________

MONDAY

TUESDAY

WEDNESDAY

THURSDAY

FRIDAY

SATURDAY

SUNDAY

TO DO

- [ ] Post on Social Media at least 3xs
- [ ] Complete Touch Point Activity
- [ ] Add Contacts to Database
- [ ] Ask for Referrals
- [ ] Review Goals
- [ ] Refer Another Business
- [ ] Plan For Next Week

SPHERE OF INFLUENCE CALLS

1.
2.
3.
4.
5.

NOTES

WEEKLY PLANNER

Week 15

Date________

MONDAY

TUESDAY

WEDNESDAY

THURSDAY

FRIDAY

SATURDAY

SUNDAY

TO DO

- [ ] Post on Social Media at least 3xs
- [ ] Complete Touch Point Activity
- [ ] Add Contacts to Database
- [ ] Ask for Referrals
- [ ] Review Goals
- [ ] Refer Another Business
- [ ] Plan For Next Week

SPHERE OF INFLUENCE CALLS

1.
2.
3.
4.
5.

NOTES

WEEKLY PLANNER

Week 16

Date________

MONDAY

TUESDAY

WEDNESDAY

THURSDAY

FRIDAY

SATURDAY

SUNDAY

TO DO

- [ ] Post on Social Media at least 3xs
- [ ] Complete Touch Point Activity
- [ ] Add Contacts to Database
- [ ] Ask for Referrals
- [ ] Review Goals
- [ ] Refer Another Business
- [ ] Plan For Next Week

SPHERE OF INFLUENCE CALLS

1.
2.
3.
4.
5.

NOTES

WEEKLY PLANNER

Week 17

Date________

MONDAY

TUESDAY

WEDNESDAY

THURSDAY

FRIDAY

SATURDAY

SUNDAY

TO DO

- [ ] Post on Social Media at least 3xs
- [ ] Complete Touch Point Activity
- [ ] Add Contacts to Database
- [ ] Ask for Referrals
- [ ] Review Goals
- [ ] Refer Another Business
- [ ] Plan For Next Week

SPHERE OF INFLUENCE CALLS

1.
2.
3.
4.
5.

NOTES

WEEKLY PLANNER

Week 18

Date________

MONDAY

TUESDAY

WEDNESDAY

THURSDAY

FRIDAY

SATURDAY

SUNDAY

TO DO

- [ ] Post on Social Media at least 3xs
- [ ] Complete Touch Point Activity
- [ ] Add Contacts to Database
- [ ] Ask for Referrals
- [ ] Review Goals
- [ ] Refer Another Business
- [ ] Plan For Next Week

SPHERE OF INFLUENCE CALLS

1.
2.
3.
4.
5.

NOTES

WEEKLY PLANNER

Week 19

Date________

MONDAY

TUESDAY

WEDNESDAY

THURSDAY

FRIDAY

SATURDAY

SUNDAY

TO DO

- [ ] Post on Social Media at least 3xs
- [ ] Complete Touch Point Activity
- [ ] Add Contacts to Database
- [ ] Ask for Referrals
- [ ] Review Goals
- [ ] Refer Another Business
- [ ] Plan For Next Week

SPHERE OF INFLUENCE CALLS

1.
2.
3.
4.
5.

NOTES

WEEKLY PLANNER

Week 20

Date________

MONDAY

TUESDAY

WEDNESDAY

THURSDAY

FRIDAY

SATURDAY

SUNDAY

TO DO

- [ ] Post on Social Media at least 3xs
- [ ] Complete Touch Point Activity
- [ ] Add Contacts to Database
- [ ] Ask for Referrals
- [ ] Review Goals
- [ ] Refer Another Business
- [ ] Plan For Next Week

SPHERE OF INFLUENCE CALLS

1.
2.
3.
4.
5.

NOTES

WEEKLY PLANNER

Week 21

Date________

MONDAY

TUESDAY

WEDNESDAY

THURSDAY

FRIDAY

SATURDAY

SUNDAY

TO DO

- [ ] Post on Social Media at least 3xs
- [ ] Complete Touch Point Activity
- [ ] Add Contacts to Database
- [ ] Ask for Referrals
- [ ] Review Goals
- [ ] Refer Another Business
- [ ] Plan For Next Week

SPHERE OF INFLUENCE CALLS

1.
2.
3.
4.
5.

NOTES

WEEKLY PLANNER

Week 22

Date________

MONDAY

TUESDAY

WEDNESDAY

THURSDAY

FRIDAY

SATURDAY

SUNDAY

TO DO

- [ ] Post on Social Media at least 3xs
- [ ] Complete Touch Point Activity
- [ ] Add Contacts to Database
- [ ] Ask for Referrals
- [ ] Review Goals
- [ ] Refer Another Business
- [ ] Plan For Next Week

SPHERE OF INFLUENCE CALLS

1.
2.
3.
4.
5.

NOTES

WEEKLY PLANNER

Week 23

Date________

MONDAY

TUESDAY

WEDNESDAY

THURSDAY

FRIDAY

SATURDAY

SUNDAY

TO DO

- [ ] Post on Social Media at least 3xs
- [ ] Complete Touch Point Activity
- [ ] Add Contacts to Database
- [ ] Ask for Referrals
- [ ] Review Goals
- [ ] Refer Another Business
- [ ] Plan For Next Week

SPHERE OF INFLUENCE CALLS

1.
2.
3.
4.
5.

NOTES

WEEKLY PLANNER

Week 24

Date________

MONDAY

TUESDAY

WEDNESDAY

THURSDAY

FRIDAY

SATURDAY

SUNDAY

TO DO

- [ ] Post on Social Media at least 3xs
- [ ] Complete Touch Point Activity
- [ ] Add Contacts to Database
- [ ] Ask for Referrals
- [ ] Review Goals
- [ ] Refer Another Business
- [ ] Plan For Next Week

SPHERE OF INFLUENCE CALLS

1.
2.
3.
4.
5.

NOTES

WEEKLY PLANNER

Week 25

Date________

MONDAY

TUESDAY

WEDNESDAY

THURSDAY

FRIDAY

SATURDAY

SUNDAY

TO DO

- [ ] Post on Social Media at least 3xs
- [ ] Complete Touch Point Activity
- [ ] Add Contacts to Database
- [ ] Ask for Referrals
- [ ] Review Goals
- [ ] Refer Another Business
- [ ] Plan For Next Week

SPHERE OF INFLUENCE CALLS

1.
2.
3.
4.
5.

NOTES

WEEKLY PLANNER

Week 26

Date________

MONDAY

TUESDAY

WEDNESDAY

THURSDAY

FRIDAY

SATURDAY

SUNDAY

TO DO

- [ ] Post on Social Media at least 3xs
- [ ] Complete Touch Point Activity
- [ ] Add Contacts to Database
- [ ] Ask for Referrals
- [ ] Review Goals
- [ ] Refer Another Business
- [ ] Plan For Next Week

SPHERE OF INFLUENCE CALLS

1.
2.
3.
4.
5.

NOTES

Quarter 2 Recap

What worked well?

Which activity did you feel most comfortable performing? Why?

Which activity was the least comfortable? Why?

Was it difficult or easy asking for referrals? Why?

How many referral leads did you receive over the past quarter?

Did you meet any new service partners you can refer to your sphere?

Did your database grow?

What adjustments need to be made for the next quarter?

Quarter 3
Planner

QUARTER 3 OPPORTUNITIES

Plan Opportunities to Touch Your Sphere of Influence in Advance

CELEBRATIONS
(Birthdays, Anniversaries, Weddings etc.)

HOLIDAYS
(Cards, Gifts, Care Packages etc)

SOCIAL MEDIA MARKETING
(Closings, New Listings, Open Houses)

PLANNED TOPICS FOR BLOG POSTS, NEWSLETTERS, EMAILS

MISCELLANEOUS TASKS

RECIPE: Quarter Activities

Remember: C = Core & P = Your Pick

Touch Goal ⟶ At Least 16 Touches A Quarter

Social Media	Direct Mail	Personal Touch
Email & Text	**Database**	**Community Involvement**

WEEKLY PLANNER

Week 27

Date________

MONDAY

TUESDAY

WEDNESDAY

THURSDAY

FRIDAY

SATURDAY

SUNDAY

TO DO

- [ ] Post on Social Media at least 3xs
- [ ] Complete Touch Point Activity
- [ ] Add Contacts to Database
- [ ] Ask for Referrals
- [ ] Review Goals
- [ ] Refer Another Business
- [ ] Plan For Next Week

SPHERE OF INFLUENCE CALLS

1.
2.
3.
4.
5.

NOTES

WEEKLY PLANNER

Week 28

Date________

MONDAY

TUESDAY

WEDNESDAY

THURSDAY

FRIDAY

SATURDAY

SUNDAY

TO DO

- [ ] Post on Social Media at least 3xs
- [ ] Complete Touch Point Activity
- [ ] Add Contacts to Database
- [ ] Ask for Referrals
- [ ] Review Goals
- [ ] Refer Another Business
- [ ] Plan For Next Week

SPHERE OF INFLUENCE CALLS

1.
2.
3.
4.
5.

NOTES

WEEKLY PLANNER

Week 29

Date________

MONDAY

TUESDAY

WEDNESDAY

THURSDAY

FRIDAY

SATURDAY

SUNDAY

TO DO

- [ ] Post on Social Media at least 3xs
- [ ] Complete Touch Point Activity
- [ ] Add Contacts to Database
- [ ] Ask for Referrals
- [ ] Review Goals
- [ ] Refer Another Business
- [ ] Plan For Next Week

SPHERE OF INFLUENCE CALLS

1.
2.
3.
4.
5.

NOTES

WEEKLY PLANNER

Week 30

Date________

MONDAY

TUESDAY

WEDNESDAY

THURSDAY

FRIDAY

SATURDAY

SUNDAY

TO DO

- [ ] Post on Social Media at least 3xs
- [ ] Complete Touch Point Activity
- [ ] Add Contacts to Database
- [ ] Ask for Referrals
- [ ] Review Goals
- [ ] Refer Another Business
- [ ] Plan For Next Week

SPHERE OF INFLUENCE CALLS

1.
2.
3.
4.
5.

NOTES

WEEKLY PLANNER

Week 31

Date________

MONDAY

TUESDAY

WEDNESDAY

THURSDAY

FRIDAY

SATURDAY

SUNDAY

TO DO

- [ ] Post on Social Media at least 3xs
- [ ] Complete Touch Point Activity
- [ ] Add Contacts to Database
- [ ] Ask for Referrals
- [ ] Review Goals
- [ ] Refer Another Business
- [ ] Plan For Next Week

SPHERE OF INFLUENCE CALLS

1.
2.
3.
4.
5.

NOTES

WEEKLY PLANNER

Week 32

Date________

MONDAY

TUESDAY

WEDNESDAY

THURSDAY

FRIDAY

SATURDAY

SUNDAY

TO DO

- [ ] Post on Social Media at least 3xs
- [ ] Complete Touch Point Activity
- [ ] Add Contacts to Database
- [ ] Ask for Referrals
- [ ] Review Goals
- [ ] Refer Another Business
- [ ] Plan For Next Week

SPHERE OF INFLUENCE CALLS

1.
2.
3.
4.
5.

NOTES

WEEKLY PLANNER

Week 33

Date________

MONDAY

TUESDAY

WEDNESDAY

THURSDAY

FRIDAY

SATURDAY

SUNDAY

TO DO

- [ ] Post on Social Media at least 3xs
- [ ] Complete Touch Point Activity
- [ ] Add Contacts to Database
- [ ] Ask for Referrals
- [ ] Review Goals
- [ ] Refer Another Business
- [ ] Plan For Next Week

SPHERE OF INFLUENCE CALLS

1.
2.
3.
4.
5.

NOTES

WEEKLY PLANNER

Week 34

Date________

MONDAY

TUESDAY

WEDNESDAY

THURSDAY

FRIDAY

SATURDAY

SUNDAY

TO DO

- [ ] Post on Social Media at least 3xs
- [ ] Complete Touch Point Activity
- [ ] Add Contacts to Database
- [ ] Ask for Referrals
- [ ] Review Goals
- [ ] Refer Another Business
- [ ] Plan For Next Week

SPHERE OF INFLUENCE CALLS

1.
2.
3.
4.
5.

NOTES

WEEKLY PLANNER

Week 35

Date________

MONDAY

TUESDAY

WEDNESDAY

THURSDAY

FRIDAY

SATURDAY

SUNDAY

TO DO

- [ ] Post on Social Media at least 3xs
- [ ] Complete Touch Point Activity
- [ ] Add Contacts to Database
- [ ] Ask for Referrals
- [ ] Review Goals
- [ ] Refer Another Business
- [ ] Plan For Next Week

SPHERE OF INFLUENCE CALLS

1.
2.
3.
4.
5.

NOTES

WEEKLY PLANNER

Week 36

Date________

MONDAY

TUESDAY

WEDNESDAY

THURSDAY

FRIDAY

SATURDAY

SUNDAY

TO DO

- [ ] Post on Social Media at least 3xs
- [ ] Complete Touch Point Activity
- [ ] Add Contacts to Database
- [ ] Ask for Referrals
- [ ] Review Goals
- [ ] Refer Another Business
- [ ] Plan For Next Week

SPHERE OF INFLUENCE CALLS

1.
2.
3.
4.
5.

NOTES

WEEKLY PLANNER

Week 37

Date________

MONDAY

TUESDAY

WEDNESDAY

THURSDAY

FRIDAY

SATURDAY

SUNDAY

TO DO

- [ ] Post on Social Media at least 3xs
- [ ] Complete Touch Point Activity
- [ ] Add Contacts to Database
- [ ] Ask for Referrals
- [ ] Review Goals
- [ ] Refer Another Business
- [ ] Plan For Next Week

SPHERE OF INFLUENCE CALLS

1.
2.
3.
4.
5.

NOTES

WEEKLY PLANNER

Week 38

Date________

MONDAY

TUESDAY

WEDNESDAY

THURSDAY

FRIDAY

SATURDAY

SUNDAY

TO DO

- [ ] Post on Social Media at least 3xs
- [ ] Complete Touch Point Activity
- [ ] Add Contacts to Database
- [ ] Ask for Referrals
- [ ] Review Goals
- [ ] Refer Another Business
- [ ] Plan For Next Week

SPHERE OF INFLUENCE CALLS

1.
2.
3.
4.
5.

NOTES

WEEKLY PLANNER

Week 39

Date________

MONDAY

TUESDAY

WEDNESDAY

THURSDAY

FRIDAY

SATURDAY

SUNDAY

TO DO

- [ ] Post on Social Media at least 3xs
- [ ] Complete Touch Point Activity
- [ ] Add Contacts to Database
- [ ] Ask for Referrals
- [ ] Review Goals
- [ ] Refer Another Business
- [ ] Plan For Next Week

SPHERE OF INFLUENCE CALLS

1.
2.
3.
4.
5.

NOTES

Quarter 3 Recap

What worked well?

Which activity did you feel most comfortable performing? Why?

Which activity was the least comfortable? Why?

Was it difficult or easy asking for referrals? Why?

How many referral leads did you receive over the past quarter?

Did you meet any new service partners you can refer to your sphere?

Did your database grow?

What adjustments need to be made for the next quarter?

Quarter 4 Planner

QUARTER 4 OPPORTUNITIES

Plan Opportunities to Touch Your Sphere of Influence in Advance

CELEBRATIONS
(Birthdays, Anniversaries, Weddings etc.)

HOLIDAYS
(Cards, Gifts, Care Packages etc)

SOCIAL MEDIA MARKETING
(Closings, New Listings, Open Houses)

PLANNED TOPICS FOR BLOG POSTS, NEWSLETTERS, EMAILS

MISCELLANEOUS TASKS

RECIPE: Quarter Activities

Remember: C = Core & P = Your Pick

Touch Goal ⟶ At Least 16 Touches A Quarter

Social Media	Direct Mail	Personal Touch
Email & Text	**Database**	**Community Involvement**

WEEKLY PLANNER

Week 40

Date________

MONDAY

TUESDAY

WEDNESDAY

THURSDAY

FRIDAY

SATURDAY

SUNDAY

TO DO

- [ ] Post on Social Media at least 3xs
- [ ] Complete Touch Point Activity
- [ ] Add Contacts to Database
- [ ] Ask for Referrals
- [ ] Review Goals
- [ ] Refer Another Business
- [ ] Plan For Next Week

SPHERE OF INFLUENCE CALLS

1.
2.
3.
4.
5.

NOTES

WEEKLY PLANNER

Week 41

Date________

MONDAY

TUESDAY

WEDNESDAY

THURSDAY

FRIDAY

SATURDAY

SUNDAY

TO DO

- [ ] Post on Social Media at least 3xs
- [ ] Complete Touch Point Activity
- [ ] Add Contacts to Database
- [ ] Ask for Referrals
- [ ] Review Goals
- [ ] Refer Another Business
- [ ] Plan For Next Week

SPHERE OF INFLUENCE CALLS

1.
2.
3.
4.
5.

NOTES

WEEKLY PLANNER

Week 42

Date________

MONDAY

TUESDAY

WEDNESDAY

THURSDAY

FRIDAY

SATURDAY

SUNDAY

TO DO

- [ ] Post on Social Media at least 3xs
- [ ] Complete Touch Point Activity
- [ ] Add Contacts to Database
- [ ] Ask for Referrals
- [ ] Review Goals
- [ ] Refer Another Business
- [ ] Plan For Next Week

SPHERE OF INFLUENCE CALLS

1.
2.
3.
4.
5.

NOTES

WEEKLY PLANNER

Week 43

Date________

MONDAY

TUESDAY

WEDNESDAY

THURSDAY

FRIDAY

SATURDAY

SUNDAY

TO DO

- [ ] Post on Social Media at least 3xs
- [ ] Complete Touch Point Activity
- [ ] Add Contacts to Database
- [ ] Ask for Referrals
- [ ] Review Goals
- [ ] Refer Another Business
- [ ] Plan For Next Week

SPHERE OF INFLUENCE CALLS

1.
2.
3.
4.
5.

NOTES

WEEKLY PLANNER

Week 44

Date________

MONDAY

TUESDAY

WEDNESDAY

THURSDAY

FRIDAY

SATURDAY

SUNDAY

TO DO

- [ ] Post on Social Media at least 3xs
- [ ] Complete Touch Point Activity
- [ ] Add Contacts to Database
- [ ] Ask for Referrals
- [ ] Review Goals
- [ ] Refer Another Business
- [ ] Plan For Next Week

SPHERE OF INFLUENCE CALLS

1.
2.
3.
4.
5.

NOTES

WEEKLY PLANNER

Week 45

Date________

MONDAY

TUESDAY

WEDNESDAY

THURSDAY

FRIDAY

SATURDAY

SUNDAY

TO DO

- [ ] Post on Social Media at least 3xs
- [ ] Complete Touch Point Activity
- [ ] Add Contacts to Database
- [ ] Ask for Referrals
- [ ] Review Goals
- [ ] Refer Another Business
- [ ] Plan For Next Week

SPHERE OF INFLUENCE CALLS

1.
2.
3.
4.
5.

NOTES

WEEKLY PLANNER

Week 46

Date________

MONDAY

TUESDAY

WEDNESDAY

THURSDAY

FRIDAY

SATURDAY

SUNDAY

TO DO

- [ ] Post on Social Media at least 3xs
- [ ] Complete Touch Point Activity
- [ ] Add Contacts to Database
- [ ] Ask for Referrals
- [ ] Review Goals
- [ ] Refer Another Business
- [ ] Plan For Next Week

SPHERE OF INFLUENCE CALLS

1.
2.
3.
4.
5.

NOTES

WEEKLY PLANNER

Week 47

Date________

MONDAY

TUESDAY

WEDNESDAY

THURSDAY

FRIDAY

SATURDAY

SUNDAY

TO DO

- [ ] Post on Social Media at least 3xs
- [ ] Complete Touch Point Activity
- [ ] Add Contacts to Database
- [ ] Ask for Referrals
- [ ] Review Goals
- [ ] Refer Another Business
- [ ] Plan For Next Week

SPHERE OF INFLUENCE CALLS

1.
2.
3.
4.
5.

NOTES

WEEKLY PLANNER

Week 48

Date________

MONDAY

TUESDAY

WEDNESDAY

THURSDAY

FRIDAY

SATURDAY

SUNDAY

TO DO

- [ ] Post on Social Media at least 3xs
- [ ] Complete Touch Point Activity
- [ ] Add Contacts to Database
- [ ] Ask for Referrals
- [ ] Review Goals
- [ ] Refer Another Business
- [ ] Plan For Next Week

SPHERE OF INFLUENCE CALLS

1.
2.
3.
4.
5.

NOTES

WEEKLY PLANNER

Week 49

Date________

MONDAY

TUESDAY

WEDNESDAY

THURSDAY

FRIDAY

SATURDAY

SUNDAY

TO DO

- [ ] Post on Social Media at least 3xs
- [ ] Complete Touch Point Activity
- [ ] Add Contacts to Database
- [ ] Ask for Referrals
- [ ] Review Goals
- [ ] Refer Another Business
- [ ] Plan For Next Week

SPHERE OF INFLUENCE CALLS

1.
2.
3.
4.
5.

NOTES

WEEKLY PLANNER

Week 50

Date________

MONDAY

TUESDAY

WEDNESDAY

THURSDAY

FRIDAY

SATURDAY

SUNDAY

TO DO

- [ ] Post on Social Media at least 3xs
- [ ] Complete Touch Point Activity
- [ ] Add Contacts to Database
- [ ] Ask for Referrals
- [ ] Review Goals
- [ ] Refer Another Business
- [ ] Plan For Next Week

SPHERE OF INFLUENCE CALLS

1.
2.
3.
4.
5.

NOTES

WEEKLY PLANNER

Week 51

Date________

MONDAY

TUESDAY

WEDNESDAY

THURSDAY

FRIDAY

SATURDAY

SUNDAY

TO DO

- [ ] Post on Social Media at least 3xs
- [ ] Complete Touch Point Activity
- [ ] Add Contacts to Database
- [ ] Ask for Referrals
- [ ] Review Goals
- [ ] Refer Another Business
- [ ] Plan For Next Week

SPHERE OF INFLUENCE CALLS

1.
2.
3.
4.
5.

NOTES

WEEKLY PLANNER

Week 52

Date________

MONDAY

TUESDAY

WEDNESDAY

THURSDAY

FRIDAY

SATURDAY

SUNDAY

TO DO

- [ ] Post on Social Media at least 3xs
- [ ] Complete Touch Point Activity
- [ ] Add Contacts to Database
- [ ] Ask for Referrals
- [ ] Review Goals
- [ ] Refer Another Business
- [ ] Plan For Next Week

SPHERE OF INFLUENCE CALLS

1.
2.
3.
4.
5.

NOTES

Quarter 4 Recap

What worked well?

Which activity did you feel most comfortable performing? Why?

Which activity was the least comfortable? Why?

Was it difficult or easy asking for referrals? Why?

How many referral leads did you receive over the past quarter?

Did you meet any new service partners you can refer to your sphere?

Did your database grow?

What adjustments need to be made for the next quarter?

52 Week Recap

You have had 52 weeks to work the plan.
Let's see how your hard work paid off!

Business Plan Review

1. What was your financial goal at the beginning of the year?
2. What were your actual earnings?

Sphere of Influence Growth

1. How many contacts did you have at the beginning of the year?
2. How many contacts did you have after 52 weeks?

Referral Business

1. How many referrals did you receive?
2. How many referrals did you convert to sales?
3. How much of your earnings were from referrals?

Get Ready For Next Year

1. What is your financial goal for next year?
2. How many referrals are you seeking for next year?

Use the goal worksheet to plan for next year.

Pick up "Recipe for Referrals" the complete planning workbook!

CONGRATULATIONS!!

Keep building your referral based business!

Made in United States
Orlando, FL
04 November 2026

90204430R00055